Get Wise

Racism and Prejudice

⇒ why is it wrong?

WOODMILL HIGH SCHOOL

Jane Bingham

Heinemann
LIBRARY

www.heinemann.co.uk/library
Visit our website to find out more information about **Heinemann Library** books.

To order:
☎ Phone 44 (0) 1865 888066
🖹 Send a fax to 44 (0) 1865 314091
💻 Visit the Heinemann Bookshop at www.heinemann.co.uk/library to browse our catalogue and order online.

First published in Great Britain by Heinemann Library, Halley Court, Jordan Hill, Oxford OX2 8EJ, part of Harcourt Education.

Heinemann is a registered trademark of Harcourt Education Ltd.

Editorial: Lucy Thunder and Harriet Milles
Design: David Poole and Kamae Design
Illustrations: Jeff Anderson
Picture Research: Melissa Allison and Kay Altwegg
Production: Camilla Smith

Originated by Ambassador Litho Ltd
Printed and bound in China, by WKT Company Limited

The paper used to print this book comes from sustainable resources.

ISBN 0 431 21033 0
08 07 06 05 04
10 9 8 7 6 5 4 3 2 1

British Library Cataloguing in Publication Data
Bingham, Jane
Get Wise – Racism and Prejudice – why is it wrong?
305.8

A full catalogue record for this book is available from the British Library.

Acknowledgements
The Publishers would like to thank the following for permission to reproduce photographs:
p. **4** Alamy/Photofusion Picture Library; p. **5** Bubbles/Angela Hampton; p. **6** Corbis/Michael Prince; p. **7** www.John Birdsall.co.uk; p. **8** Action Plus/Glyn Kirk; pp. **9**, **17** Alamy/Image 100; p. **11** Alamy Images; p. **12** Bubbles/John Powell; p. **13** Alamy/Sarkis Images; p. **14** Topham Picturepoint; p. **16** Corbis/Richard T. Nowitz; p. **18** Bananastock/Alamy; p. **19** Bubbles; pp. **20**, **26** Action Plus/Neil Tingle; p. **21** Corbis Sygma/Bradford T&A; p. **22** Hulton Archive; p. **23** Bettmann/Corbis; p. **24** Getty/Hulton; p. **25** Corbis/David Turnley; p. **29** Alamy/David Young-Wolff

Talk time images pp. **9**, **10**, **27**, **29** Getty Images/Photodisc

Cover photograph reproduced with permission of Reuters/Paul Hackett

The Publishers would like to thank Dr Ute Navidi, former Head of Policy with ChildLine, for her assistance in the preparation of this book.

Every effort has been made to contact copyright holders of any material reproduced in this book. Any omissions will be rectified in subsequent printings if notice is given to the Publishers.

Important note: If you are experiencing racism or prejudice and need help, go straight to the Getting help box on page 31. There are phone numbers to call for immediate help and support.

Contents

Words appearing in bold, **like this**, are explained in the Glossary.

What are racism and prejudice?

What does it mean to be prejudiced or racist?

Next time you walk down the street, take a good look at the people around you. Are they all the same age, size and height? Do they all have the same hairstyle and skin colour? Of course not! Everyone is different – and that is what makes life interesting.

Snap judgments

Sometimes, people are mean to others just because they look different, or behave differently from them. They decide that they don't like certain people, without ever bothering to get to know them. When people make snap judgments like this, they are being prejudiced.

Prejudice comes in many forms. People can be prejudiced against others because of their age, their size, their sex, or even because they have a disability.

The world is full ➲ of a huge variety of people. Most of the time, they all get on very well together.

Racism

Some people are prejudiced against others because they or their family come from a different country, because they have a different skin colour, or because they have a different way of life. This kind of prejudice is called racism.

Racism often involves making fun of people, turning them into 'outsiders', and **bullying** them. Sometimes people are beaten up or even killed in **racist attacks**. Racism is against the **law** in countries such as the UK and Australia.

Nobody should have to suffer from prejudice, and everyone has the **right** to be treated fairly and equally. This book will look at the reasons why some people are prejudiced. It will also help you cope with prejudice and racism.

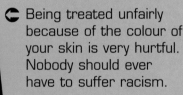

Being treated unfairly because of the colour of your skin is very hurtful. Nobody should ever have to suffer racism.

Not like me?

Why are some people racist and prejudiced – and should you ever follow their example?

Some people decide straightaway that they won't like a person – just because he or she is different from them. Of course they are wrong. They are also missing out on some great friendships. So what makes people think like this?

It's not what I'm used to

Some people like to stick to what they know. They can't imagine what it would be like to come from another country or to have a different way of life. So they only choose friends who seem just like them.

One of the reasons why people do this is because they don't feel confident in new situations. But if they made the effort to get to know different people, their lives would be much more interesting and fun.

Follow the leader

People who are prejudiced learn their attitudes from others. They might hear other people making racist statements at school, in the street or on television. Or perhaps a member of their family has racist views. It is very easy to copy what other people say without ever thinking things through for yourself.

Sometimes you might hear adults expressing racist views, but that does not mean you should ever copy them.

Think for yourself

Prejudiced people often take a very one-sided view. They may say things like 'girls are stupid' or 'old people are boring'. These one-sided pictures are called **stereotypes**. If you think it through for yourself, it is easy to see that these statements are untrue. Everyone is different and each person is an **individual** with his or her own character.

THINK IT THROUGH

Is there ever an excuse for being prejudiced?

Yes. You can't be friends with people who are different from you.

No. You should see someone as a real person, not a stereotype.

What do YOU think?

◖ Getting to know people from different cultures can be interesting and fun. Don't be scared of differences – enjoy them!

7

Odd one out

Why do some people keep others out – and how does it feel to be left out?

Some people show their prejudice by keeping others out of their group. They make these people feel like 'outsiders' – very unwelcome and different. This can be extremely hurtful if you are the one being left out.

Not in our gang

People are always forming groups. Some groups are organized, like sports teams or clubs. Others are just groups of friends who like to meet up to have fun and chat. Being part of a group can feel great, but sometimes people in groups don't treat others well. If they decide that someone doesn't 'fit in' they can be very cruel to that person.

You wouldn't understand

Group members can find many excuses for keeping people out. They may say that the person who wants to join their group would not understand what they like to talk about, or enjoy the same sports. In many cases, they are wrong. If they would just give new people more of a chance, they would discover that they could be valuable members of the group, too.

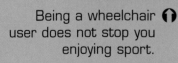

Being a wheelchair ⌒ user does not stop you enjoying sport.

Out in the cold

Being kept out of a group can make you feel very lonely and angry. Why should you be left out, just because you are not exactly the same as the others? And why can't you have the chance to show what you could add to the group?

Talk time

Have you ever been left out?

Rick: My step-brother tells me I'm too young to talk to him and his mates.

Lei-Lei: The boys say girls can't play football, so they won't let me join in.

Scott: Some kids at school keep me out of their gang because I'm not white like them.

Tanvi: Yeah, that's happened to me as well. It made me feel really angry.

Jason's story

Jason has always been a wheelchair user – but he is also a champion table-tennis player, and a keen football supporter:

'The boys at my school always left me out when they were talking about football. I felt really bad. Just because I'm in a wheelchair, it doesn't mean I'm not interested in sport! Then, one day, someone saw in the paper that I'd won a table-tennis competition. Now the other boys play table tennis with me – although I always beat them! I've also started going to football matches with them.'

THINK IT THROUGH

Should you ever leave someone out of your group?

Yes. If someone is different, they won't fit into the group.

No. They might have interesting things to add to the group.

What do YOU think?

🎧 All sorts of different people like talking about fashion.

Making fun?

What's so funny about being cruel to people?

People who are racist or prejudiced often make fun of others and call them names. This may seem like harmless fun, but it is no joke when you are the one who is being laughed at.

Fun and games?

When people meet someone who is different from them, they may make fun of the way this person looks, speaks, or dresses. Or they may tell jokes about their **race** or religion, or even their disability.

> You can't come with us. You've got stupid-looking shoes!

Talk time

Have you ever been made fun of?

Rick: Some people laugh at me because I'm small for my age, and I'm no good at spelling.

Lei-Lei: I get teased for wearing braces on my teeth.

Tanvi: People point at my dad in the street, because he wears traditional dress.

🎧 It really hurts when other people make fun of your race or religion.

Name calling

As well as making fun of others, some people call others cruel names – and even call them out in the street. Nobody should ever have to put up with this. When you call people names, you are refusing to recognize that they have the **right** to be **respected** and treated like everyone else.

It's no joke

Laughing at others is unkind and thoughtless. People can't change the way they look or talk. They may not have enough money to buy smart clothes, or they may be proud of dressing in a different way. Mocking and calling people names can sometimes be dangerous too. If someone is being laughed at all the time, they might decide to fight back – and then things can quickly get out of control.

THINK IT THROUGH

Is it ever OK to laugh at other people?

Yes. It's only a bit of fun. People should be able to take a joke.

No. Making fun of others is never a joke.

What do YOU think?

When prejudice and racism are directed towards you, it feels terrible. You may be sad, lonely and scared, or you may feel angry. All these feelings are natural, but you should not have to go through any of this.

Talking helps

Talking to someone you trust will make you feel much better, and help you to cope with what is happening to you. Think about who you could talk to – it may be a school friend, a brother or a sister.

Fact Flash

Many schools have a **school council** where pupils can talk about problems such as racism, prejudice and bullying.

Adult advice

It is very hard to put a stop to prejudice and racism on your own. You need to find someone you can trust to help you sort things out. This may be a teacher, a parent or another adult, who can take some action to solve the problem.

⟲ It's a great relief to let your feelings out and share your thoughts with someone else.

Always tell an adult if you are experiencing racism or prejudice. These are serious problems that need to be tackled.

Telling tales?

Sometimes, children who are experiencing prejudice don't want to go to a teacher or another adult, because they think this is telling tales. But prejudice and racism are always wrong and need to be stopped. It is a good idea to write down what has been said or done to you, so you can show others exactly what has happened.

Outside help

If you can't find an adult to help, or if you feel you need extra support, there are several **organizations** you can contact. Some of them have a telephone helpline to call, so you can talk to someone about your problems. You can find out how to contact these organizations on page 31.

Vijay's story

Vijay was fed up with being teased and bullied at school, so he asked a teacher for help:

'Some of the boys at school started calling me names and laughing at me. They just wouldn't leave me alone. It got to the stage when I couldn't bear it any more, so I went to my teacher. After she'd sorted out the problem, some other kids told me they'd been teased too. They were really pleased I'd asked for help.'

THINK IT THROUGH

Is it right to tell an adult if you are being bullied or teased?

Yes. Telling an adult is the best way to get the problem stopped.

No. Nobody likes a tell-tale.

What do YOU think?

What do you do when you want to fight back?

Sometimes being on the receiving end of racism or prejudice can make you feel very angry. You may even feel like hitting back. But getting into a fight is not the answer. There are much better ways of facing up to prejudice.

Seeing red

If people say unfair or hurtful things, you may want to say things back or even start a fight. This is only natural – but you should always try to control yourself. If you let prejudiced or racist people see that you have lost control, you are letting them win – and they will probably try to upset you again.

Sometimes it's hard ➲ to overcome your anger, but it feels much better when you stay in control.

What do you mean you don't want to fight?

Time out

Taking 'time out' before you speak or act will help you to take control of the situation. Instead of hitting back straightaway, give yourself some time to calm down. You may find it helps to take deep breaths or count to ten inside your head.

Taking it calmly

Once you have calmed down, you may decide that the best thing to do is simply to walk away. Or you may feel able to tell your tormentors to leave you alone. You may even feel strong enough to explain to them calmly why their views are wrong. You might find it easier to do this if you have a friend or an adult to support you.

Sam's story

Sam had been followed around the school playground by a gang of boys for days. Then he decided to take 'time out':

'They kept saying mean things about my colour and my family. I used to shout back at them and sometimes I got into a fight. But then I decided to ignore them. It was quite funny because they really didn't know what to do about it. I suppose they decided it wasn't so much fun teasing me when I wouldn't get angry, so now they leave me alone.'

THINK IT THROUGH

Is it ever right to fight back?

Yes. People who are prejudiced deserve to be hurt themselves.

No. Fighting is dangerous and always makes things worse.

What do YOU think?

Being strong

How do you stay confident when you are facing prejudice or racism?

When you experience racism or prejudice it can make you lose confidence. It is hard to feel good about yourself when other people are making fun of you. But however hard it is, you should always try to be positive. By being strong and confident, you will show the people who are trying to attack you that they just can't win.

Feeling bad

Being a **victim** of prejudice can make you feel cut off from other people. It can also make it hard to concentrate, so school work becomes difficult. Sometimes it can even lead you to stay away from school. Once you start missing school, it is much harder to feel part of a group. However, none of this has to happen.

🔊 Spending time with a favourite pet can often help you feel more positive.

Positive thinking

Positive thinking means feeling good about yourself. If other people see that you are happy with the way you are, and that you seem confident and strong, they won't try to pick on you. Always try to remember the things you like about yourself. Keep in contact with your friends and do things with them that you enjoy. You can also have plenty of fun with your pets, or with your family. Just remember there are lots of people out there who think you are great!

○ It can really help to talk things through with an older brother or sister.

TOP TIPS

It is not easy facing prejudice or racism, but here is a list of things that can help:

◎ Don't let people stop you feeling good about yourself.

◎ Take 'time out' before you speak or act.

◎ Talk to a friend about how you are feeling.

◎ Ask a trusted adult to help you stop the problem.

◎ Telephone a helpline to get more advice and support.

◎ Always remember, there is nothing wrong with you – it is your tormentors who are in the wrong.

THINK IT THROUGH

Does thinking positively really help?

Yes. If you like yourself, you can overcome a lot of problems.

No. The way you think about yourself doesn't make any difference to other people.

What do YOU think?

How can you help to put a stop to racism and prejudice?

Racism and prejudice are problems for everyone, whether they directly affect you or not. Often it is very hard for the **victims** of prejudice to speak out. Then it is up to others to make sure that everyone is treated fairly.

It's not my problem?

What do you do when people say hurtful things or behave in a way that is racist or prejudiced? Do you just pretend you haven't noticed? Or do you take some action to stop their behaviour? Obviously you should never get involved in a situation that could turn out to be dangerous – but there are still some things you can do.

⊙ Sometimes you need to tell your friends that you think what they are doing or saying is wrong.

Taking action

You may decide to tell a teacher or another adult about the situation – or even raise the problem at a **school council** meeting. If your friends are being prejudiced, you might decide to talk to them yourself. It takes a lot of courage to tell other people that you don't agree with them, but it could make them think again and change their minds.

A friend in need

When someone is being teased or treated unfairly, they really need a friend. One of the best things you can do is offer your support. Just by listening to your friend, you will make them feel much better.

TOP TIPS

Here are some things you can do to stop prejudice winning:

◎ Refuse to join in when your friends are being racist or prejudiced.
◎ Talk to your friends about why prejudice is wrong.
◎ Comfort a friend who is being teased.
◎ Tell an adult whom you trust about what is going on.

⬤ If a friend is being treated unfairly, you might offer to go with them to see an adult who could help.

T08199
305.8

THINK IT THROUGH

Does it matter if other people are prejudiced?

Yes. We should all try to take a stand against prejudice.

No. Other people can think what they like.

What do YOU think?

What can be done about racism and prejudice in society?

Sport can be a ➲ great way of bringing people together. What does it matter what colour someone is, when you are all playing for the same team?

Racism and prejudice can happen everywhere – at work, in shops and restaurants, and on the streets. Treating people differently because of their **race**, religion, disability, age or sex, is called **discrimination**. In countries like the UK and Australia there are **laws** against discrimination.

Prejudice in everyday life

Even though there are laws to prevent it, some people have to deal with prejudice every day. Staff in shops or restaurants may be rude to them, or simply ignore them, and people may make fun of them or call them names.

Some people suffer from racism and prejudice at work. They may not be offered a job in the first place, or they may not be given the chance of a better job, even though they have earned it. People who are treated unfairly at work have a **right** to demand equal treatment.

Sometimes large groups of people become angry about racism – and things can quickly get out of hand.

Trouble on the streets

Sometimes, racism can get out of hand. Fights can break out and people can be seriously hurt, or even killed. Occasionally, in some big cities, large groups of people may take to the streets. As well as upsetting many people, these **demonstrations** can sometimes turn violent.

Living together

Living and working alongside people of other races doesn't have to cause problems. In fact, it often works very well. When people spend time with each other every day, they stop seeing **stereotypes** and get to know the real person instead.

Newsflash

In some cases, racism can lead to murder. In 1993, a young black man, Stephen Lawrence, was stabbed to death on a street in London by a group of white youths. Stephen was simply waiting with a friend for a bus to take him home.

How much did people suffer from racism and prejudice in the past?

Racism and prejudice are not new problems. Throughout history, some groups of people have treated others cruelly – just because they were different from them. One of the worst examples of racism is **slavery**. The practice of slavery began thousands of years ago, and there are still slaves in some parts of the world today.

Even young children ➥ were forced to work as slaves on farms in the Americas.

Fact Flash

Between 1600 and 1800, over 11 million people were forced to leave Africa and sent to work as slaves in the Americas and West Indies.

The slave trade

In the 1580s, millions of Africans were captured and packed into ships that took them to America. One in five of them died on the journey, and those who survived were sold as slaves. Most masters worked their slaves very hard and many slaves died young.

Fighting slavery

By the 1800s, some people were starting to speak out against the slave trade. One person who fought hard against slavery was Harriet Tubman. Harriet was born into a slave family in North America, but she managed to escape. She then helped more than 300 other slaves to escape to safety.

Black rights

Long after slavery ended, people were still prejudiced against black people. Right up until the 1960s black people in the USA were not allowed the same **rights** as whites. One person who stood up for the rights of black people was Dr Martin Luther King, a black church minister. In 1963 he made an inspiring speech (see Top thoughts). The following year, the US government passed new **laws** that made it **illegal** to treat people differently because of their colour or **race**.

Top thoughts

'I have a dream that my ... children will one day live in a nation where they will not be judged by the colour of their skin but by the content of their character.'

Dr Martin Luther King, American **campaigner** for equal rights

Martin Luther King was a brilliant speaker. He made people realise that they had to change the way that black people were treated. Sadly, he was shot dead in 1968 by a racist killer.

How has racism been shown across the world – and have we learnt any lessons?

Throughout history, groups of people have been **persecuted** because of their **race** or their religion, or both. A terrible example of this took place in Europe in the last century.

The Holocaust

During World War II (1939–1945) the German Nazi party, led by Adolf Hitler, tried to wipe out the Jewish people. The Nazis believed that the Jewish race was not pure and so they wanted to get rid of it completely. They sent Jewish men, women and children to **concentration camps**, where millions of them were put to death.

The Nazis also persecuted other groups, such as gypsies and mentally handicapped people. Altogether, around 15 million people were murdered by the Nazis. This appalling tragedy is known as the **Holocaust**.

Anne Frank's story

Anne Frank and her family were persecuted by the Nazis during World War II because they were Jewish.

Anne Frank belonged to a Jewish family, living in Amsterdam in the Netherlands. They were forced to go into hiding to escape the Nazis. Anne kept a diary for two years, describing her life inside a sealed-up office building. Eventually, her family was discovered and she died in a concentration camp at the age of fifteen.

During World War II, the German Nazis packed Jewish people into trains, like cattle, and sent them to the concentration camps.

People under threat

Since the Holocaust, many other groups of people have been persecuted. During the 1990s, war broke out in Bosnia (in Eastern Europe) when the Christian Serbian people tried to drive the Muslim Kosovan people out of their lands. In Africa, millions of people have been killed in wars between tribes and races.

Keeping people safe

So, what is being done to prevent more people being persecuted? Some **organizations**, such as Amnesty International, work for the **rights** of everyone to be treated fairly and equally.

There are also **laws** against persecution laid down by the United Nations, an organization working for world peace. If a country disobeys these laws, the United Nations may decide to take action against them.

❶ During the war in Bosnia, thousands of Muslim Kosovan people were forced to leave their homes.

THINK IT THROUGH

Could something like the Holocaust ever happen again?

Yes. Some people will always be racist, no matter what.

No. Organizations and education can teach people what is wrong.

What do YOU think?

Fighting racism and prejudice

How are people standing up to different forms of prejudice?

There are many different kinds of prejudice in the world today, but **campaigners** are fighting back to make sure that everyone is treated fairly and equally. You and your friends can also make a difference (see pages 28–29).

➲ Some disabled people can achieve amazing things.

Fighting racism

One of the most famous campaigners against racism is Nelson Mandela, who has spent his adult life working for equal **rights** for black people in South Africa. In 1962, he was sent to prison for 27 years for being a member of a group that was banned by the white South African government. In 1994, Mandela became his country's first black president.

Disability rights

People with disabilities often have to fight very hard for their rights. For instance, they may not be offered certain jobs. However, in the UK and Australia it is now against the law for employers to **discriminate** against disabled people at work.

Top thoughts

'See the person, not the disability.'

Message on a poster to raise public awareness about disability

Talk time

What should be done to make things fairer for everyone?

 Tanvi: Women who stay at home to look after their families should be given more respect.

 Lei-Lei: Yeah, and girls should have the right to play football in school.

 Scott: People shouldn't lose their jobs just because they're disabled.

 Rick: Or because they're not so young any more.

Rights for women

A century ago, women in the UK were not allowed to vote in **elections**, and almost no women went to university. By the 1920s, women campaigners, known as suffragettes, had won the right for women to vote. By the 1970s, it was against the **law** in the UK and Australia to pay women less than men.

Big is beautiful

People who are larger than average often have to face teasing, name-calling and even discrimination at work. It is very hurtful and unfair to be treated differently just because of your body shape. Many people are campaigning for better treatment for larger people.

Newsflash

In some societies, elderly people face prejudice. However, since 1966, the Japanese have held a one-day holiday every year to show respect for older people. On this day, called *Keiro no Hi*, everyone recognizes the important role played by older people in society and concentrates on the rights and needs of the elderly.

How can you change things for the better?

Everyone can make a difference to the way other people are treated. The best way to start is to notice what is happening around you, and to support the people in your life.

Be aware

Try to be aware of the ways that other people are treated. If people are being prejudiced, you could (tactfully!) point it out to them – or ask an adult for help and advice. If you have experienced prejudice yourself, you will be especially good at understanding the problem. You may even be able to help your friends stand up to their tormentors.

Keep a lookout for any difficulties that other people have to face. For example, there may be areas of your school where children who use wheelchairs have problems. You could point this out to a teacher who might be able to find a **solution**.

Talk time

How do you make sure that others are treated fairly?

 Lei-Lei: I try to think about the things I say – so I don't upset people needlessly.

Rick: If my mates make racist remarks, I tell them I don't agree.

 Tanvi: Yeah, I stick up for myself – and for my friends.

Scott: Me too. But most of all – I just enjoy all my different friends.

When you forget about differences, life can be more enjoyable for everybody.

Time for a change

You, too, can help to change the world. There are many **organizations** and charities that **campaign** against prejudice and racism (see page 31 for a list). Some organizations have special websites for children where you can find out more about them. You can also raise money for charities by planning special events, like a sale or a sponsored swim.

Everybody wins

Racism and prejudice cause a lot of unhappiness. They also mean that people miss out on some great friendships. Without prejudice in their lives, people can enjoy being different and have a lot more fun together.

THINK IT THROUGH

Can you really change the way people behave?

Yes. You have to start somewhere and even little things make a difference.

No. It takes more than one person to change the way people behave.

What do YOU think?

Glossary

bully to pick on someone and treat them cruelly and unfairly

campaign work to make something happen

concentration camp prison camp set up by the Nazis in World War II, to which Jews and other prisoners were sent

demonstration public action, usually a march, to show your views about something

discriminate treat someone unfairly

election when people vote for a person, or a group, to do an important job

ethnic origin group of people or race that you originally come from

Holocaust mass murder of Jewish people, and other groups, by the Nazis during World War II

illegal against the law

individual separate person with their own character, who is not just part of a group

law rules made by the government of a country that must be obeyed

nationality country to which you belong

organization large group of people all working together to achieve the same aims

persecute treat someone cruelly and unfairly

race one of the major human groups in the world. People of the same race come originally from the same part of the world.

racist attack attack on another person or people because they belong to a different race

refugee someone who has escaped from their country because of war or other problems

respect taking someone or something seriously, and not making fun of them

right something that is fair and that everyone can expect

school council group made up of students and teachers who discuss problems in the school and try to find solutions

slavery practice of capturing people and forcing them to spend all their lives working for their masters

solution answer to a problem or a way of solving that problem

stereotype very simple and one-sided picture of a person, which doesn't show the whole individual

victim someone who suffers because of the actions of somebody else

Check it out

Check out these books and websites to find out more about racism and prejudice, and to get help and advice.

Books

The Diary of a Young Girl: Definitive Edition, Anne Frank, Otto Frank (ed.), Mirjam Pressler (ed.) (Penguin Books Ltd. 1997)

We're Different, We're The Same, Bobbi Jane Kates (Sesame Street Pictureback) (Random House, 1992)

Get Wise: Bullying, Sarah Medina (Heinemann Library, 2004)

Life and World of Anne Frank, Brian Williams (Heinemann Library, 2003)

Websites

Amnesty International (UK): www.amnesty.org.uk; (Australia) www.amensty.org.au

Commission for Racial Equality (UK): www.cre.gov.uk

Human Rights and Equal Opportunity Commission (Australia): www.hreoc.gov.au

National Society for the Prevention of Cruelty to Children (UK): www.nspcc.org.uk

---

Getting help

If you feel very worried or upset about racism or prejudice, you may want to talk to someone urgently. You can speak to an adult you trust, or phone a helpline for support.

- In the UK, you can phone ChildLine on 0800 11 11 (open 24 hours a day); textphone number 0800 400 222; or go to their website: www.childline.org.uk. Please remember that calls to 0800 numbers are free, and they do not show up on phone bills.

- In Australia, you can phone Kids Help Line on 1800 55 1800 (open 24 hours a day), or go to their website: http://www.kidshelp.com.au

Remember – you do not have to be alone.

Index

Titles in the *Get Wise* series include:

Hardback   0 431 21032 2

Hardback   0 431 21003 9

Hardback   0 431 21004 7

Hardback   0 431 21002 0

Hardback   0 431 21035 7

Hardback   0 431 21033 0

Hardback   0 431 21036 5

Hardback   0 431 21000 4

Hardback   0 431 21001 2

Hardback   0 431 21034 9

Find out about other titles from Heinemann Library on our website
www.heinemann.co.uk/library